FAVORITE FESTIVAL SOLOS

10 GREAT NFMC SELECTIONS

The **National Federation of Music Clubs (NFMC)** is a non-profit philanthropic music organization whose goal is to promote American music, performers, and composers through quality music education and supporting the highest standards of musical creativity and performance.

ISBN 978-1-4584-1771-8

WILLIS MUSIC

EXCLUSIVELY DISTRIBUTED BY

HAL•LEONARD® CORPORATION

7777 W. BLUEMOUND RD. P.O. BOX 13819 MILWAUKEE, WI 53213

© 2012 by The Willis Music Co.

Visit Hal Leonard Online at
www.halleonard.com

CONTENTS

EDITOR'S NOTE: Special thanks to Glenda Austin for providing notes on the Gillock pieces.

COSSACK DANCE / William Gillock
NFMC 1991-1994

A "cossack" is another term for a Ukrainian or Russian soldier. The original text by Gillock is as follows:

> **Cossacks dancing by the firelight, balalaikas strumming.**
> **Sabres flashing, oh, so dashing! What a thrilling sight! Oh!**
> **Boots of leather, black and shiny, move with speed and daring.**
> **Fast as lightning, so exciting, what a thrilling sight! Oh!**

This is a neatly crafted 16-measure piece that well illustrates the Ukrainian folk dance. The single note melody in Dorian mode aligns beautifully with the fact that the dance itself is usually performed as a solitary concert dance. The melody (in primarily quarter notes) transcends back and forth between the left and right hands. When the optional accompaniment is added, "Cossack Dance" becomes an exciting performance piece for both the player and the audience!

THE PYTHON / Randall Hartsell
NFMC 2004-2006

To the student:

> Read over the lyrics of this piece. Now, read the words aloud and chant the lyrics with an even quarter-note rhythm. What is the form of a snake? Can you name three major parts? Relate these parts to the form of this composition. Can you find the introduction, main theme, and coda (tail)?

> Name the key. Try playing it in C Major by not using any flats. Perhaps you can change these lyrics to be about a garter snake when you play in C Major. Ask friends which key they like best. And, be sure to play the duet with your teacher or a friend. Enjoy!

WIND IN THE BAMBOO TREE / William Gillock
NFMC 1998-2000

"Wind in the Bamboo Tree" is a lovely and delicate Asian-inspired lullaby. It is in 3 clear sections: A-B-A¹. Even though there is no B-flat in the key signature, an F Major/d minor feel is implied. The note values are simple—quarter, whole and half—which give it an even, stable mood. Melodic passing tones in the right hand gently glide over the left hand accompaniment, which is always an open fifth. Although the pedal is marked optional, I would recommend its use. Once again, Gillock has created a short, simple, and satisfying piece that delivers a sense of beauty, achievement, and fulfillment to both the player and listener.

A NEW DAY / Carolyn C. Setliff
NFMC 2004-2006

> **From the eastern sky, a new light beams,**
> **Casting color upon a blackened night.**
> **Darkness is fleeing, a new day is dawning,**
> **Sunbeams soon bring glorious light.**

The student has the opportunity to play expressively and use a wide expanse of the keyboard. The different dynamic markings, rhythmic changes, echoes in high octaves, and the left hand chromatic melody in the B section all give color to this musical picture of a "new day."

INDIAN DANCE / Carolyn Miller
NFMC 1995-1997

"Indian Dance" starts with a short introduction of open fifths between hands. The motif of the quarter note followed by two eighth notes symbolizes the deep bass drum and the smaller, higher-sounding drum. The main theme gives students a chance to practice articulation by way of two and three-note slurs, and staccatos. The middle section gives the student's right hand experience with intervals of fourths while the left hand continues with the low open fifth. "Indian Dance" is straightforward yet descriptive, and I hope students will have fun performing it.

PUNCH AND JUDY (Puppet Dance) / Eric Baumgartner
NFMC 2007-2010

Punch and Judy are puppet characters that date back to the 1600s. A Punch and Judy puppet show is often fun and lively with plenty of action and slapstick humor. Picture these playful characters as you practice. Crisp staccato, strong accents and big dynamic changes will help bring them to life!

AUTUMN IS HERE / William Gillock
NFMC 1995-1997

"Autumn Is Here" offers a poignant, sentimental meditation of the changing seasons. Gone are the hot, bright sunny days of summer—enter the cooler, beautiful, golden orange hues of the season. Perhaps a bit of nostalgia occurs in the middle section (C Major) with a brief remembrance of the past. Musically, bring out the right hand, which always has the melody (even on a cross-over section), with the left hand accompanying softly.

FIESTA FUN / Carolyn Miller
NFMC 1995-1997

"Fiesta Fun" has a catchy rhythmic pattern that makes it fun to play. Students will have the opportunity to recognize various broken chords and five-finger patterns. The staccato notes mixed with alternating legato phrases add energy. Several teachers have told me that this piece has been successful as a recital solo!

STATELY PROCESSION / William Gillock
NFMC 1995-1997

This Gillock classic is loaded with sequences, both rhythmic and melodic. Of particular interest is the triplet rhythm in the right hand—which is easy for the student because it lies perfectly under the fingers. Every note and chord is accessible, especially if the indicated fingering is observed. Gillock was an expert at doing just this: making a piece sound great, while also making it so very playable. Marked in *moderate march time*, remember not to rush—these processors are royal, elegant, and unhurried.

THE WHISKERY WALRUS / Glenda Austin
NFMC 2001-2003

Students: A walrus is a big, blubbery, brown blob with long white tusks and whiskers. They move slowly. So on this piece, do not rush. If you do, you're not a walrus!

Teachers: The melody is mostly in the bass clef, with a little bit of cross-over into the treble clef. Harmonically, there are two chords in the entire piece: I (E Major) and V^7 (B Major^7). However, in the Coda, the IV chord (A Major) provides a break in the harmonic pattern. Because of the few chord changes, this piece would be excellent for a beginner to study and analyze.

Cossack Dance

Words and Music by
William Gillock

In a spirited manner

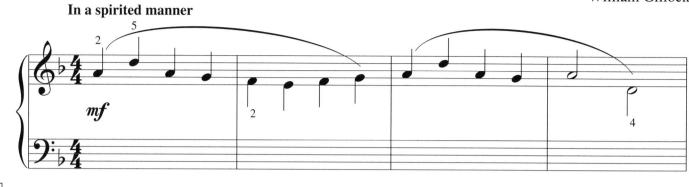

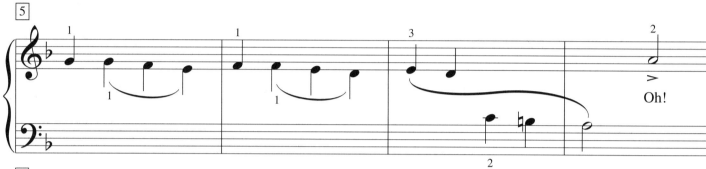

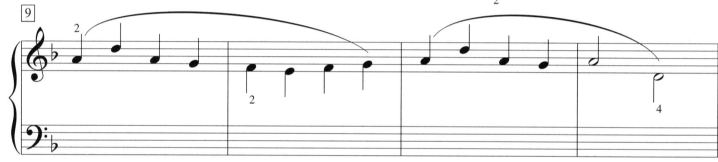

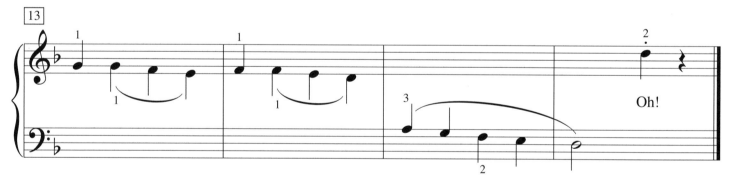

Optional Accompaniment (Student plays as written.)

In a spirited manner

Note to the teacher: "Cossack Dance" also appears in *Piano All the Way* without staccatos or accents in the solo.

The Python

Music by Randall Hartsell
Words by Janthi Fisher Webster, D.V.M.

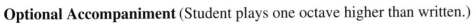

Optional Accompaniment (Student plays one octave higher than written.)

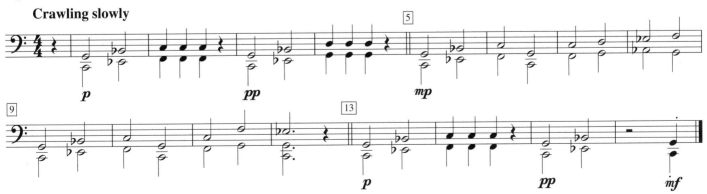

Wind in the Bamboo Tree

William Gillock

Softly, with gentle movement

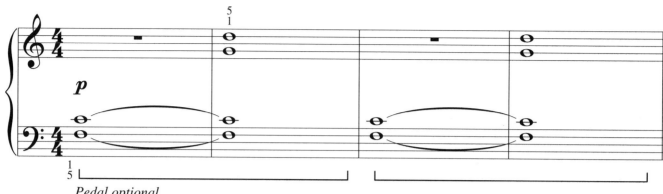

Pedal optional

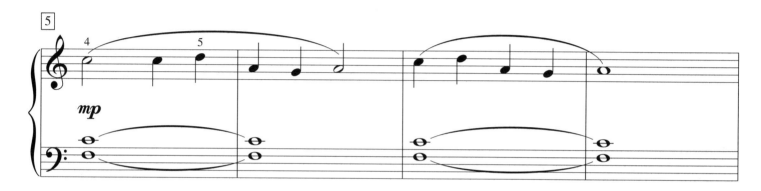

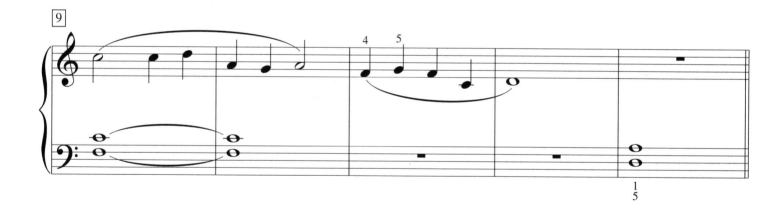

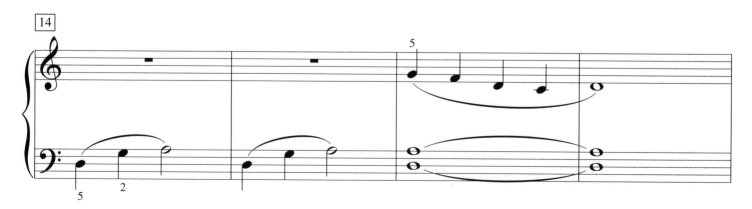

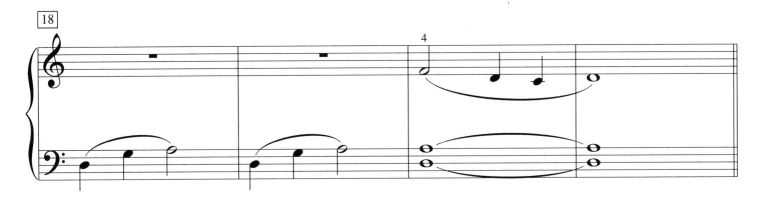

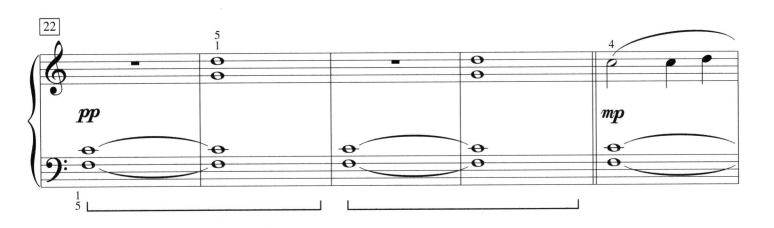

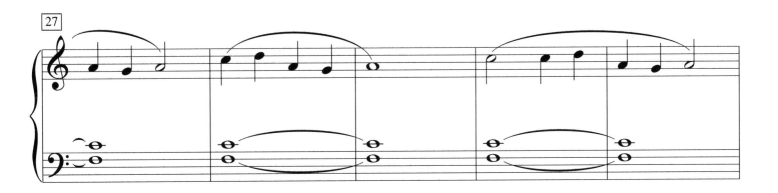

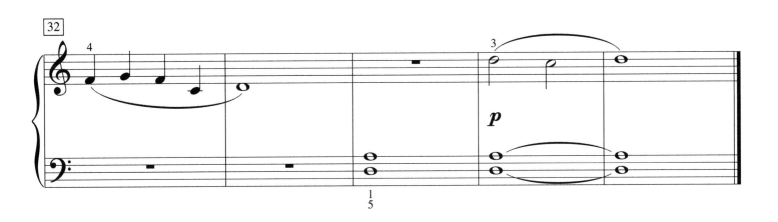

A New Day

Carolyn C. Setliff
Revised by David Engle

Indian Dance

Carolyn Miller

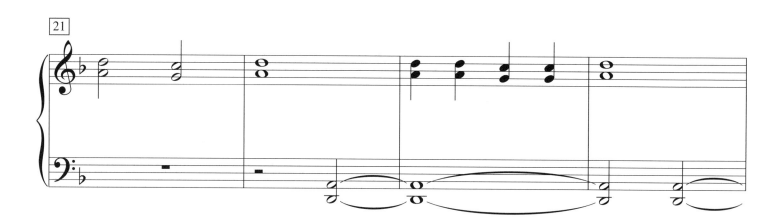

For Brittany and Diamond

Punch and Judy
(Puppet Dance)

Eric Baumgartner

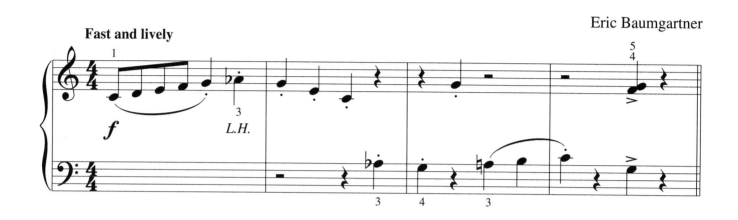

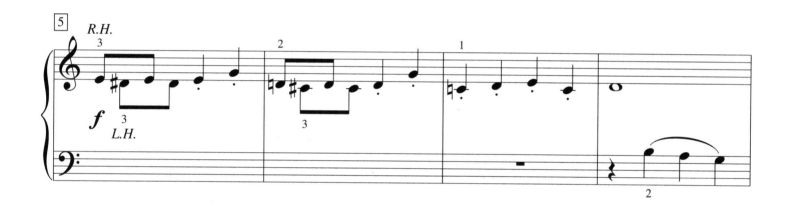

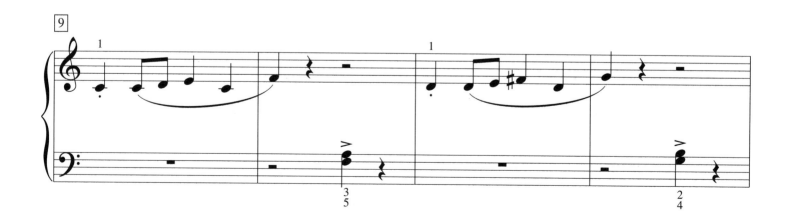

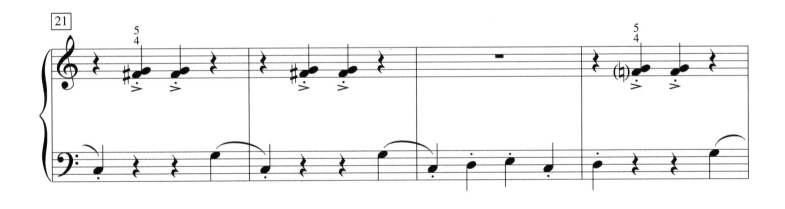

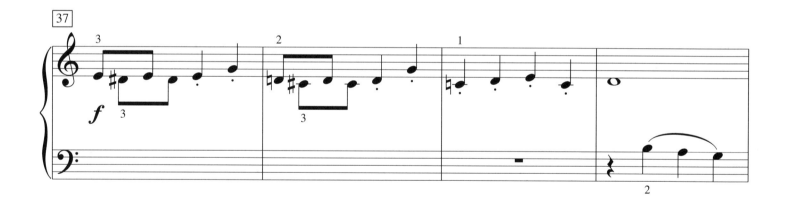

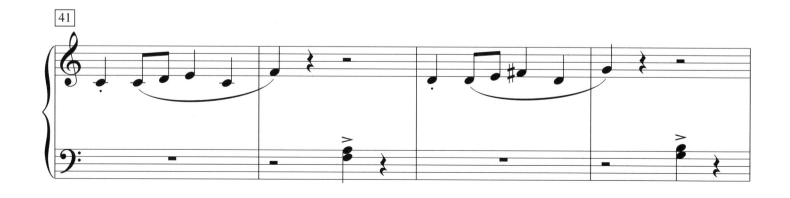

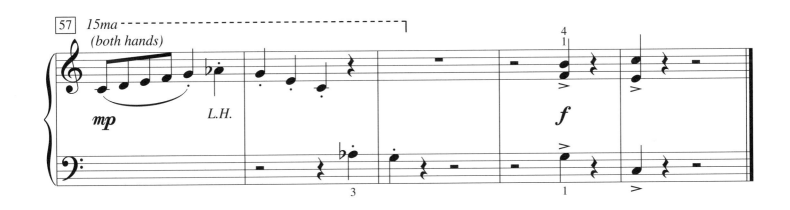

Autumn Is Here

William Gillock

Slowly, with a singing tone

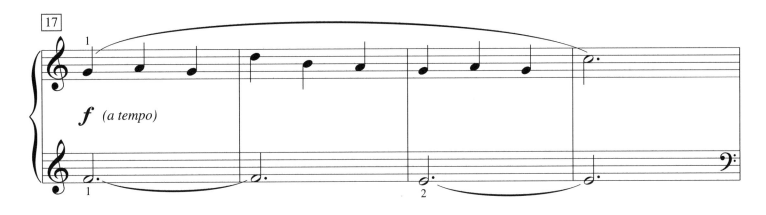

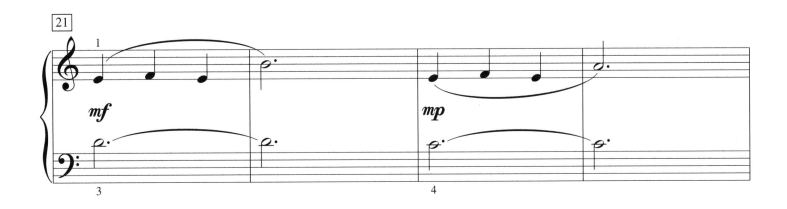

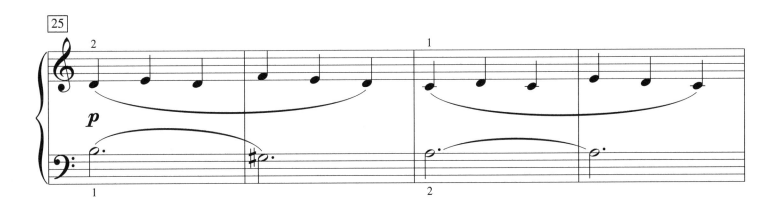

D.C. al Fine

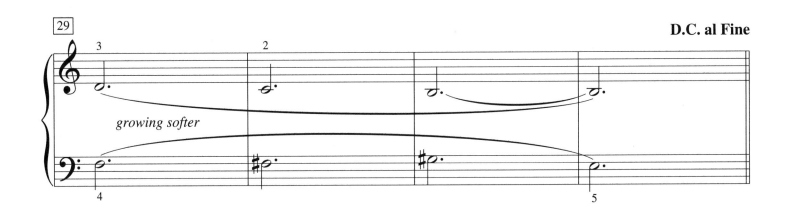

growing softer

Fiesta Fun

Carolyn Miller

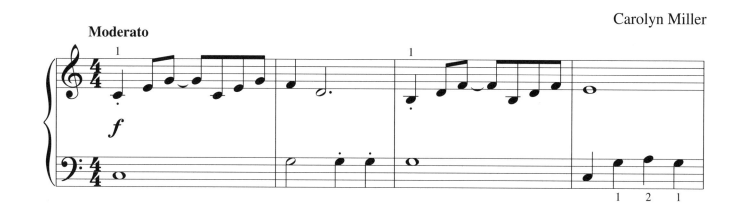

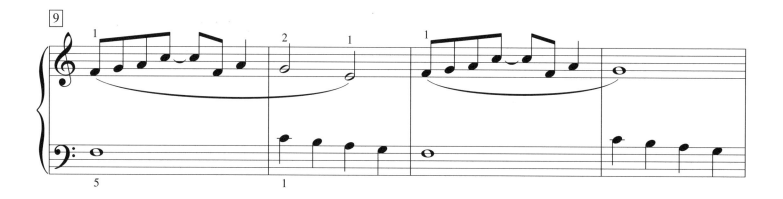

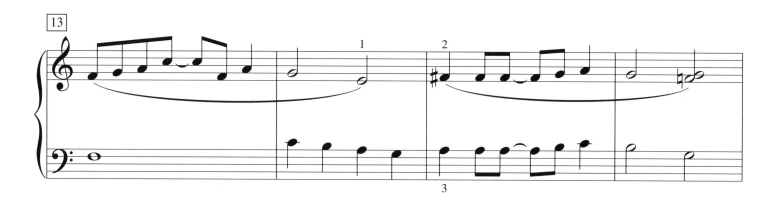

To Robert Douglas

Stately Procession

William Gillock

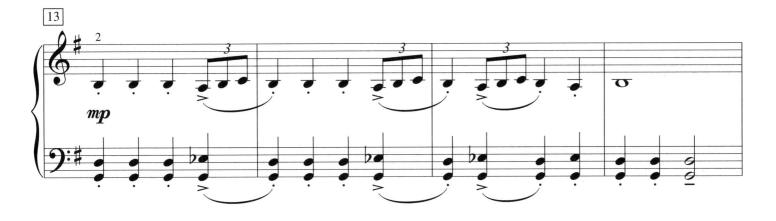

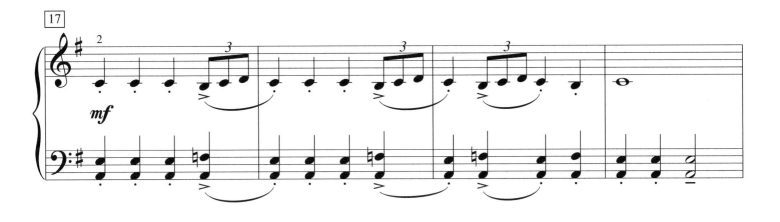

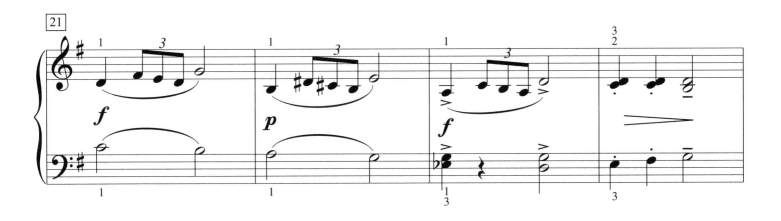

The Whiskery Walrus

Glenda Austin

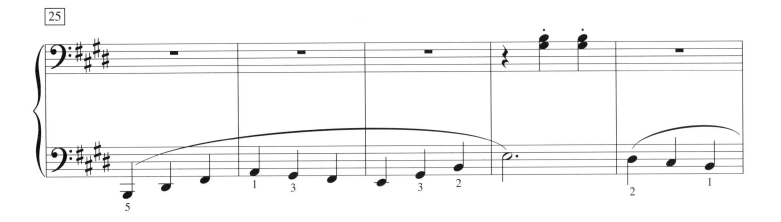

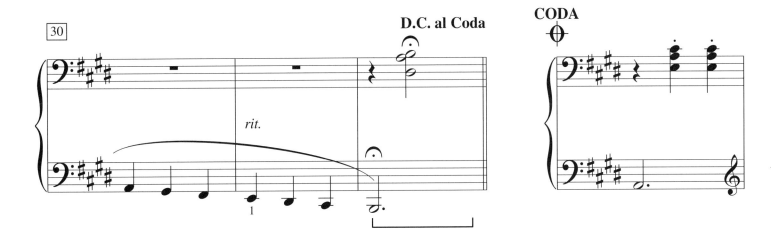

A DOZEN A DAY

by Edna Mae Burnam

The **A Dozen A Day** books are universally recognized as one of the most remarkable technique series on the market for all ages! Each book in this series contains short warm-up exercises to be played at the beginning of each practice session, providing excellent day-to-day training for the student. The CD is playable on any CD player and features fabulous backing tracks by Ric Iannone. For Windows® and Mac users, the CD is enhanced so you can access MIDI files for each exercise and adjust the tempo.

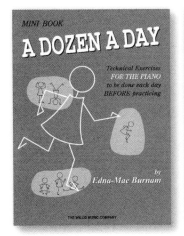
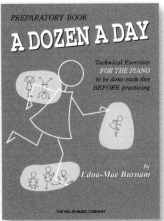
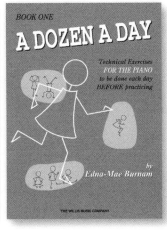
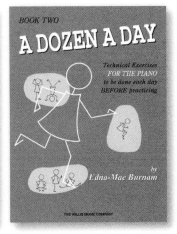

MINI BOOK
00404073 Book Only $3.99
00406472 Book/CD..........................$8.99

PREPARATORY BOOK
00414222 Book Only $3.99
00406476 Book/CD..........................$8.99

BOOK 1
00413366 Book Only $3.99
00406481 Book/CD..........................$8.99

BOOK 2
00413826 Book Only $3.99
00406485 Book/CD..........................$8.99

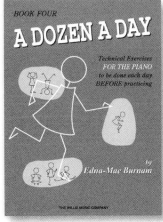

BOOK 3
00414136 Book Only $4.99
00416760 Book/CD..........................$9.99

BOOK 4
00415686 Book Only $5.99
00416761 Book/CD......................$10.99

PLAY WITH EASE IN MANY KEYS
00416395 Book Only $3.95

WILLIS MUSIC

EXCLUSIVELY DISTRIBUTED BY

HAL•LEONARD®

Prices, contents, and availability subject to change without notice. Prices listed in U.S. funds.

Dynamic Duets
and Exciting Ensembles from Willis Music!

SELECTED COLLECTIONS*

00416804 Accent on Duets (MI-LI) /
          William Gillock..........................$12.99
00416822 All-American Ragtime Duets
          (EI) / *Glenda Austin* $7.99
00416732 Concerto No. 1
          for Piano and Strings (MI) (2P, 4H) /
          Alexander Peskanov $14.95
00416931 Contest Duets & Trios (EE-LE).. $7.99

* 1 Piano, 4 Hands, unless otherwise indicated.

SELECTED SHEETS

Early Elementary
00406709 Flying (1P, 4H) / *Carolyn Miller*.. $2.50
00406743 Wisteria (1P, 4H) /
          Carolyn C. Setliff.........................$2.95

Mid-Elementary
00412289 Andante Theme from
          "Surprise Symphony" (1P, 8H) /
          Haydn, arr. Bilbro $2.95
00406208 First Jazz (1P, 4H) /
          Melody Bober.............................$2.50
00406789 Little Concertino in C (1P, 4H) /
          Alexander Peskanov $2.95
00411777 Song of the Rain (2P, 4H) /
          Dorothy Gaynor Blake $1.95

Later Elementary
00415178 Changing Places (1P, 4H) /
          Edna Mae Burnam $2.95
00405427 Happy, Happy Dance (1P, 4H) /
          David Karp.................................$1.95
00406209 Puppy Pranks (1P, 4H) /
          Melody Bober.............................$2.50
00416864 Rockin' Ragtime Boogie (1P, 4H) /
          Glenda Austin.............................$3.99

Early Intermediate
00416754 Bouquet (1P, 4H) / *Naoko Ikeda* $3.95
00416716 Bravo Brasilia! (1P, 4H) /
          Glenda Austin.............................$3.95
00416843 Festive Celebration (1P, 4H) /
          Carolyn Miller $3.99
00416734 Fifth Avenue Stroll (1P, 4H) /
          Glenda Austin.............................$3.95
00412287 Hungarian Dance No. 5 (1P, 4H) /
          Brahms, arr. Wallis.....................$2.95
00416854 A Little Bit of Bach (1P, 4H) /
          Glenda Austin $3.99
00416529 A Little Salsa in Tulsa (1P, 4H) /
          Glenda Austin $3.50
00414710 Solfeggietto (2P, 4H) / *CPE Bach,
          arr. Van Hulse*............................$1.95
00416921 Tango in D Minor (IP, 4H) / *Carolyn
          Miller*...$3.99

00416898 Duets in Color Book 1 (EI-MI) /
          Naoko Ikeda $12.99
00416899 Duets in Color Book 2 (EI-MI) /
          Naoko Ikeda $12.99
00406230 First Piano Duets (EE) /
          John Thompson series $4.95
00416805 New Orleans Jazz Styles Duets
          (EI) / *Gillock, arr. Austin*............$9.99
00416668 Pandora (EI) / *Naoko Ikeda*........$4.95
00416830 Teaching Little Fingers Easy Duets
          (EE) / *arr. Miller* $5.99

Mid-Intermediate
00406141 Amazing Grace (1P, 4H) /
          arr. Kaplan $2.95
00411831 Ave Maria (2P, 4H) /
          Bach-Gounod, arr. Hinman........$2.95
00410726 Carmen Overture (1P, 6H) /
          Bizet, arr. Sartorio......................$3.95
00404388 Champagne Toccata (2P, 8H) /
          William Gillock $3.95
00416762 Country Rag (2P, 4H) /
          Alexander Peskanov $4.95
00405212 Dance of the Sugar Plum Fairy /
          Tchaikovsky, arr. Gillock............ $3.99
00405657 Valse Elegante (1P, 4H) /
          Glenda Austin $3.95

Later Intermediate
00415223 Concerto Americana (2P, 4H) /
          John Thompson $5.95
00405552 España Cañi (1P, 4H) /
          Marquina, arr. Gillock $3.95
00410903 The Robin's Return (1P, 4H) /
          Fisher, arr. Niel $2.95
00405409 March of the Three Kings
          (1P, 4H) / *Bizet, arr. Gillock*.......$2.95

Advanced
00411832 Air (2P, 4H) / *Bach,
          arr. Hinman* $2.95
00405154 Dallas Tango (1P, 4H) /
          David Karp.................................$2.95
00405663 Habañera (1P, 4H) /
          Stephen Griebling $2.95
00405299 Jesu, Joy of Man's Desiring
          (1P, 4H) / *Bach, arr. Gillock*.......$3.95
00405648 Pavane (1P, 4H) /
          Fauré, arr. Carroll......................$2.95

CLOSER LOOK

View sample pages and
hear audio excerpts online at
www.halleonard.com.

FOR MORE INFORMATION, SEE YOUR LOCAL MUSIC DEALER,
OR WRITE TO:

HAL•LEONARD®
CORPORATION
7777 W. BLUEMOUND RD. P.O. BOX 13819 MILWAUKEE, WI 53213

Prices, contents, and availability subject to change without notice.

Spectacular Piano Solos

from

www.willispianomusic.com

Early Elementary

00416850	Barnyard Strut/*Glenda Austin*	$2.99
00416702	Big Green Frog/*Carolyn C. Setliff*	$2.99
00416904	The Blizzard/*Glenda Austin*	$2.99
00416882	Bow-Wow Blues/*Glenda Austin*	$2.99
00416883	Catch Me!/*Frank Levin*	$2.99
00406670	Cookies/*Carolyn Miller*	$2.95
00404218	Fog at Sea/*William Gillock*	$2.95
00416907	Guardian Angels/*Naoko Ikeda*	$2.99
00416918	Halloween Surprise/*Ronald Bennett*	$2.99
00412099	Moccasin Dance/*John Thompson*	$1.95
00416783	My Missing Teeth/*Carolyn C. Setliff*	$2.95
00416933	The Perceptive Detective/*Carolyn Miller*	$2.99
00416816	Rain, Rain/*Carolyn Miller*	$2.99

Mid-Elementary

00416780	The Acrobat/*Carolyn Miller*	$2.99
00416041	Autumn Is Here/*William Gillock*	$2.99
00416902	Cherokee Prayer of Peace/*Glenda Austin*	$2.99
00416803	The Dancing Bears/*Carolyn Miller*	$2.99
00405925	Gentle Breeze/*Carolyn Miller*	$2.99
00416878	Mini Toccata/*Eric Baumgartner*	$2.99
00404738	Moonlight/*William Gillock*	$2.95
00416728	Seahorse Serenade/*Carolyn C. Setliff*	$2.95
00416674	Seaside Dancer/*Ronald Bennett*	$2.50
00416785	Watermelon Sunset/*Randall Hartsell*	$2.95

Later Elementary

00416840	At The Ballet/*Carolyn C. Setliff*	$2.99
00416852	Black Cat Chat/*Eric Baumgartner*	$2.99
00416887	Chromatic Craze/*Carolyn C. Setliff*	$2.99
00416786	Egyptian Journey/*Randall Hartsell*	$2.95
00416906	Evening Melody/*Naoko Ikeda*	$2.99
00416886	Flying Fingers/*Carolyn C. Setliff*	$2.99
00416836	The Gentle Brook/*Carolyn Miller*	$2.99
00416908	The Goblins Gather/*Frank Levin*	$2.99
00416747	Halloween Hop/*Al Rita*	$2.95
00405918	Monkey on a Stick/*Lynn Freeman Olson*	$2.95
00416866	October Leaves/*Carolyn C. Setliff*	$2.99
00406552	Parisian Waltz/*Robert Donahue*	$2.95
00416781	The Race Car/*Carolyn Miller*	$2.95
00416664	Roses in Twilight/*Carolyn C. Setliff*	$2.95
00416885	Scaling the Peaks/*Randall Hartsell*	$2.99
00406564	Showdown/*Ronald Bennett*	$2.95
00416919	Sparkling Waterfall/*Carolyn C. Setliff*	$2.99
00416820	Star Wonders/*Randall Hartsell*	$2.99
00416779	Sunrise at San Miguel/*Ronald Bennett*	$2.99
00416913	Sunshine Spectacular/ *Randall Hartsell*	$2.99
00416828	Tick Tock/*Eric Baumgartner*	$2.99
00416881	Twilight Tarantella/*Glenda Austin*	$2.99

Early Intermediate

00405455	Bass Train Boogie/*Stephen Adoff*	$2.99
00416817	Broken Arm Blues/*Carolyn Miller*	$2.99
00416841	The Bubbling Brook/*Carolyn Miller*	$2.99
00416849	Bye-Bye Blues/*Glenda Austin*	$2.99
00416945	Cafe Francais/*Jonathan Maiocco*	$2.99
00416834	Canopy of Stars/*Randall Hartsell*	$2.99
00415585	Flamenco/*William Gillock*	$2.95
00416856	Garden of Dreams/*Naoko Ikeda*	$2.99
00416703	The Joplin Jubilee Rag/*Glenda Austin*	$2.95
00416818	Majestic Splendor/*Carolyn C. Setliff*	$2.99

00416733	The Matador/*Carolyn Miller*	$2.99
00416942	A Melancholy Night/*Naoko Ikeda*	$2.99
00416877	Mystic Quest/*Randall Hartsell*	$2.99
00416873	Le Papillon (The Butterfly)/*Glenda Austin*	$2.99
00416829	Scherzo Nuovo/*Eric Baumgartner*	$2.99
00416937	Stampede/*Carolyn Miller*	$2.99
00416917	Supernova/*Ronald Bennett*	$2.99
00416842	Tarantella In G Minor/*Glenda Austin*	$2.99
00416782	Toccata Caprice/*Carolyn C. Setliff*	$2.95
00416938	Toccatina Tag/*Ronald Bennett*	$2.99
00416869	Twilight Tapestry/*Randall Hartsell*	$2.99
00416681	Vista/*Ronald Bennett*	$2.50
00416924	A Waltz to Remember/*Glenda Austin*	$2.99

Mid-Intermediate

00416698	Black Key Blues/*Alexander Peskanov*	$2.95
00416911	Blues Streak/*Eric Baumgartner*	$2.99
00416855	Dance of the Unicorn/*Naoko Ikeda*	$2.99
00416893	Fantasia in A Minor/*Randall Hartsell*	$2.99
00416821	Foggy Blues/*Naoko Ikeda*	$2.99
00414908	Fountain in the Rain/*William Gillock*	$2.95
00416800	The Glacial Mermaid/*Naoko Ikeda*	$2.95
00416765	Grand Sonatina in G/*Glenda Austin*	$2.95
00416875	Himalayan Grandeur/*Randall Hartsell*	$2.99
00416700	Intermezzo in B Minor/*arr. Frank Levin*	$2.95
00406630	Jazz Suite No. 2/*Glenda Austin*	$3.95
00416910	Little Rock (& Roll)/*Eric Baumgartner*	$2.99
00416939	Midnight Fantasy/*Carolyn C. Setliff*	$2.99
00416857	Moonlight Rose/*Naoko Ikeda*	$2.99
00414627	Portrait of Paris/*William Gillock*	$1.95
00405171	Sea Nocturne/*Glenda Austin*	$2.99
00416844	Sea Tempest/*Randall Hartsell*	$2.99
00415517	Sonatine/*William Gillock*	$2.99
00416701	Spanish Romance/*arr. Frank Levin*	$2.95
00416100	Three Jazz Preludes/*William Gillock*	$3.95
00416726	Tumbling Toccatina/*Claudette Hudelson*	$2.99
00416801	Two Romances/*Naoko Ikeda*	$3.95

Later Intermediate

00416715	Hear the Spirit of America/*Marilyn Briant and Andrew Zatman*	$2.95
00416764	Romantic Rhapsody/*Glenda Austin*	$2.95
00405646	Soft Lights/*Carolyn Jones Campbell*	$1.95
00409464	Tarantella/*A. Pieczonka*	$2.95

Early Advanced

00415263	Impromptu/*Mildred T. Souers*	$2.95
00415166	Sleighbells in the Snow/*William Gillock*	$2.95
00405264	Valse Brillante/*Glenda Austin*	$2.95

FOR MORE INFORMATION, SEE YOUR LOCAL MUSIC DEALER,
OR WRITE TO:

HAL•LEONARD® CORPORATION

7777 W. BLUEMOUND RD. P.O. BOX 13819 MILWAUKEE, WI 53213

CLOSER LOOK View sample pages and hear audio excerpts online at www.halleonard.com

  www.facebook.com/willispianomusic

Prices & availability subject to change without notice.

MUSIC FROM
William Gillock

Available exclusively from WILLIS MUSIC

"The Gillock name spells magic to teachers around the world..."
Lynn Freeman Olson, renowned piano pedagogue

NEW ORLEANS JAZZ STYLES

Gillock believed that every student's musical education should include experiences in a variety of popular stylings, including jazz, as a recurring phase of his or her studies. Students should also be encouraged to deviate from the written notes with their own improvisations if desired, for spontaneity is an essential ingredient of the jazz idiom.

Originals

NEW ORLEANS JAZZ STYLES
00415931 Book Only...$4.99

MORE NEW ORLEANS JAZZ STYLES
00415946 Book Only...$4.99

STILL MORE NEW ORLEANS JAZZ STYLES
00404401 Book Only...$4.99

NEW ORLEANS JAZZ STYLES - COMPLETE
00416922 Book/CD $19.99

Duets (arr. Glenda Austin)

NEW ORLEANS JAZZ STYLES DUETS
00416805 Book/CD $9.99

MORE NEW ORLEANS JAZZ STYLES DUETS
00416806 Book/CD $9.99

STILL MORE NEW ORLEANS JAZZ STYLES DUETS
00416807 Book/CD $9.99

Simplified (arr. Glenda Austin)

SIMPLIFIED NEW ORLEANS JAZZ STYLES
00406603 ....$5.99

MORE SIMPLIFIED NEW ORLEANS JAZZ STYLES
00406604 ....$5.99

STILL MORE SIMPLIFIED NEW ORLEANS JAZZ STYLES
00406605 ....$5.99

PIANO – ALL THE WAY!

Piano – All the Way! is a multi-key course of study written and composed for the beginning piano pupil. It is designed to present the fundamental concepts of theory and literature in a wide variety of styles, leading to musical understanding and independent reading.

00405273	Level 1A Book	$6.95
00416252	Level 1B Book	$6.95
00415943	Level 2 Book	$6.95
00415944	Level 3 Book	$6.95
00415945	Level 4 Book	$6.95

TECHNIC – ALL THE WAY!

00404213	Level 1A Book	$2.25
00404214	Level 1B Book	$2.25
00404460	Level 2A Book	$2.50
00404895	Level 2B Book	$2.95

THEORY – ALL THE WAY!

00416347	Level 1A Book	$2.95
00416348	Level 1B Book	$2.95
00404084	Level 2A Book	$4.50
00404085	Level 2B Book	$2.95

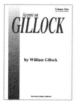

ACCENT ON GILLOCK SERIES

Excellent piano solos in all levels by Gillock. Great recital pieces!

00405993	Volume 1 Book	$4.99
00405994	Volume 2 Book	$4.99
00405995	Volume 3 Book	$4.99
00405996	Volume 4 Book	$4.99
00405997	Volume 5 Book	$4.99
00405999	Volume 6 Book	$4.99
00406000	Volume 7 Book	$4.99
00406001	Volume 8 Book	$4.99

"ACCENT ON" SERIES

Selections of original early to mid-intermediate level piano solos, each with a specific pedagogical focus.

00415712	Accent on Analytical Sonatinas	EI	$4.99
00415797	Accent on Black Keys	MI	$3.95
00416932	Accent on Classical	EI-MI	$7.99
00416804	Accent on Duets	MI-LI	$12.99
00415748	Accent on Majors	LE	$4.95
00415569	Accent on Majors & Minors	EI	$4.99
00415165	Accent on Rhythm & Style	MI	$3.95

ALSO AVAILABLE

FOUNTAIN IN THE RAIN

A sophisticated Gillock classic! Composed in 1960, this piece is reminiscent of impressionism and continues to be on annual recital lists. Students particularly enjoy the changing harmonies and nailing the splashy cadenza in the middle!
00414908..$2.95

PORTRAIT OF PARIS

This beautiful composition evokes the romance of long-ago Paris, its eighth notes building gracefully to an incredibly satisfying climax of cascading notes. Excellent for bringing out top-voicing. Gillock has also written a second piano part that results in a very effective piano duo arrangement. (Second Piano Part: 00416293)
00414627..$2.99

THREE JAZZ PRELUDES

These preludes may be played as a set or as individual pieces. These dazzling pieces are Gillock at his best.
00416100..$3.95

CLASSIC PIANO REPERTOIRE – WILLIAM GILLOCK

12 beautiful Gillock pieces have been re-engraved in this new collection that is guaranteed to be well-worn in no time! Renowned piano pedagogue Lynn Freeman Olson once wrote: "The Gillock name spells magic to teachers around the world… In each Gillock composition, no matter what the teaching purpose, music quality comes first." Includes favorites such as *Valse Etude, Festive Piece, Polynesian Nocturne,* and *Sonatine.*
00416912...$12.99

Prices, contents, and availability subject to change without notice.

WILLIS MUSIC

FOR MORE INFORMATION, SEE YOUR LOCAL MUSIC DEALER, OR WRITE TO:

HAL•LEONARD® CORPORATION
7777 W. BLUEMOUND RD. P.O. BOX 13819 MILWAUKEE, WI 53213

Find us online at
www.willispianomusic.com

www.facebook.com/willispianomusic